tapas

tapas

a culinary journey of discovery

SUSANNA TEE

Love Food ™ is an imprint of Parragon Books Ltd

Parragon
Queen Street House
4 Queen Street
Bath BA1 1HE, UK

ISBN: 978-1-4054-9251-5
Printed in China

Produced by the Bridgewater Book Company Ltd

Photography: Laurie Evans
Home economist: Carol Tennant

Notes for the Reader
This book uses imperial, metric, and US cup measurements. Follow the same units of measurement throughout; do not mix imperial and metric. All spoon measurements are level: teaspoons are assumed to be 5 ml, and tablespoons are assumed to be 15 ml. Unless otherwise stated, milk is assumed to be whole, eggs and individual vegetables such as potatoes are medium, and pepper is freshly ground black pepper. Recipes using raw or very lightly cooked eggs should be avoided by infants, the elderly, pregnant women, convalescents, and anyone suffering from an illness. The times given are an approximate guide only.

Picture Acknowledgements
The publisher would like to thank the following for permission to reproduce copyright material: Neo Vision/Getty (page 12), Bilic/photocuisine/Corbis (page 33), Brigitte Sporrer/zefa/Corbis (page 38), Poisson d'Avril/photocuisine/Corbis (page 54) and Chris Everard/Stone/Getty (page 74).

Contents

Introduction

Tapa means a "cover" or "lid," and this gives us a clue to how this cuisine began. Perhaps it was a glass of wine or sherry being covered by a slice of bread, or maybe by a saucer with a slice of bread, ham, or a few olives on it, to keep out the fruit flies, dust, or rain. This led to the bread being eaten, which led to the bread becoming something more substantial and a way for the bar owner to tempt his customers and increase his wine sales. Bowls of salted nuts, marinated olives, anchovies, artichoke hearts, a cube of Manchego or the local cheese, and slices of *jamón serrano* (cured ham) or chorizo sausage are the simplest of tapas. Over the years, these little helpings of food have become an enormous repertoire of small dishes. There are small portions of deep-fried fish and vegetables, a pan of sizzling shrimp, meatballs, croquettes, *pinchos* (small kabobs or tapas on toothpicks), wedges of tortilla (Spanish omelet), stuffed eggs, cooked dishes in a sauce to be shared among friends and, of course, delicious concoctions piled on top of bread or toast.

Eating tapas with a glass of wine, sherry, or cold beer before a meal, both at lunchtime and in the evening, is a way of life in Spain. *Tapeo,* "the art of eating tapas," is an informal social occasion that gives people from all walks of life the opportunity to chat and have a snack. It is usually eaten standing up at a bar or *tasca*, and often people spend the evening strolling from bar to bar on a gastronomic tapas crawl. The idea is that these small helpings stimulate your appetite before a meal, which is then followed by lunch or dinner. For a Spaniard, tapas are rarely eaten to take the place of a meal. In

Spain, *una tapa* is a small single serving, often only a mouthful or two, while *una ración* is a more substantial portion, equivalent to a small entrée, which serves four as a tapa. A *media ración* (half portion) serves two. In bars, the simplest tapas such as olives and nuts may still be included in the price of the drink. When it comes to paying, trust often prevails, or at bars where the tapas are served on toothpicks the waiter will count up the number of empty sticks.

Serving tapas at home

Despite tapas being traditionally eaten in bars and taverns, and designed to precede a meal, a selection of tapas dishes can be served as a meal in itself. Tapas are ideal for a summer lunch or supper party and lend themselves to an informal, enjoyable social occasion. In addition, they can be prepared for a small handful of guests or a large buffet. The dishes are easy to prepare and many can be prepared in advance. For a meal, serve about eight different types of dishes and accompany with a salad or two. Choose at least one tapa from each chapter in this book so that you have a combination of bread, fish, meat, and vegetables. Try to choose a mixture of hot and cold dishes using a variety of cooking styles.

With your selection of dishes, include bowls of the simplest tapas, which would not be complete without a bowl of olives, since Spain has the largest olive-producing industry in the world, as well as being the largest producer and exporter of olive oil. Choose from the wide selection available, such as green, black, pitted or with the pits left in, *manzanilla*, crushed (*machacadas*), large queen (*gordales*), stuffed (*rellenas*), and flavored (*aliñades*). In addition, serve with breadsticks and lots of crusty bread to soak up the juices. If you wish to serve a dessert, then fresh fruit such as grapes, figs, and wedges of melon would be a good choice.

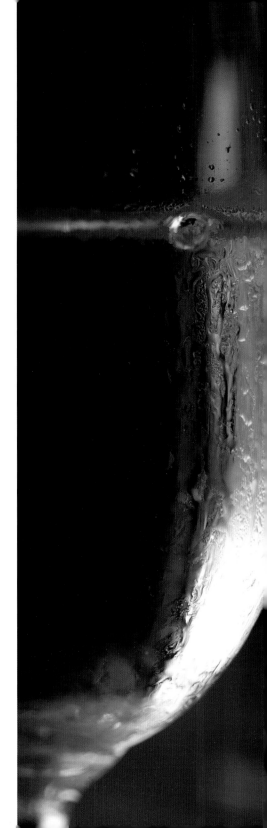

For a truly authentic touch, serve the dishes in small round, brown glazed earthenware dishes, known as *cazuela*, typically used in tapas bars, as they retain the heat well. Most tapas, because of their bite-size servings, are eaten with the fingers, or failing that, a fork or a toothpick, but never knives. Some less elegant Spanish bars cover their floors in sawdust in expectation of it being strewn with discarded napkins, toothpicks, olive pits, and shrimp shells by the end of the evening. When entertaining at home, provide plates, depending on the occasion, plenty of napkins for wiping sticky fingers, and a bowl for discarded toothpicks.

A glass of something fortifying

While red and/or white wine or beer may be the obvious choice of drink to accompany tapas at home, eating tapas also goes hand in hand with a glass of sherry. Sherry is a fortified wine with a high alcoholic content. Outside Spain, it is served as an aperitif before dinner, but in Spain, a light dry fino sherry is drunk throughout the meal as a white wine. Spanish sherry is produced in Andalusia, where it is always served with tapas. In fact, it is here that in the 19th century the tapa is claimed to have originated and some would say where the best tapas are to be found.

There is a variety of sherries, ranging from very dry aperitif wines to very sweet dessert wines. Fino is Spain's finest white wine and is the least alcoholic type. It is pale in color, light and dry, and always served chilled. Manzanilla, also a fino, is slightly sweeter; amontillado, which is fino that has been matured in barrels, is softer and darker, and is often slightly sweet; and oloroso is deep red in color, rich and fruity, and usually sweeter. Cream sherry is made by blending oloroso sherry with sweet red wines. It is dark and rich, and typically accompanies desserts.

Sangria

Another drink that makes a good alternative to serving wine or beer with tapas is Spanish sangria. Sangria is normally made from red wine, and its name derives from the word *sangre*, meaning "blood," because of its appearance. It is straightforward to make at home and makes a wonderful summer's drink. It can be made with white wine if you prefer, when it is known as *sangria blanco* (white sangria).

Sangria

Serves 12–15

4 oranges
6 lemons
generous ⅓ cup Spanish brandy
generous ¾ cup superfine sugar
2 x 25.4 fl oz/750 ml bottles Spanish red wine, chilled
ice cubes, to serve

Squeeze the juice from 2 of the oranges and 3 of the lemons and put the juice in a nonreactive bowl. Add the brandy and cover, then let infuse and chill in the refrigerator for at least 2 hours.

Meanwhile, slice and quarter the remaining fruit. Put in a bowl, then cover and chill in the refrigerator until required.

To serve, pour the fruit juice and brandy into a large serving pitcher. Add the sugar and chilled wine and stir until the sugar has dissolved. Serve topped with the prepared fruit and plenty of ice cubes.

Tinto de Verano

As an alternative to sangria, you could serve this lighter drink, which is a variation of sangria. Omit the brandy and put the fruit juice, prepared fruit, and ice cubes in a large serving pitcher, then add 1 bottle of chilled red wine. Top off with an equal quantity of chilled sparkling lemonade and stir well to mix.

Allioli

The recipe that you will turn to time and time again is Allioli, or garlic mayonnaise, the ubiquitous sauce served in Catalan tapas bars as a dip for all sorts of different tapas. The word Allioli comes from the Catalan words *all i oli* (garlic and oil)—the original recipe was made with only these two ingredients and a pinch of salt. The absence of egg yolks made it different from the French *aïoli*, but because the Spanish recipe was hard to make egg yolks were eventually added. This means that today, the only difference between the Spanish and French recipes is in the spelling. Nowadays there are also recipes that thicken and flavor the sauce with bread, boiled potatoes, honey, nuts, or tomatoes.

In Spain, Allioli is easily bought from food stores, but it can also be prepared at home with fresh eggs or commercially made mayonnaise. The version made with eggs is considered by some to have a superior taste, but as it contains raw egg, it should not be served to infants, the elderly, pregnant women, convalescents, and anyone suffering from an illness. Making it with commercially made mayonnaise is simpler. Once made, both can be stored in the refrigerator for up to 2 days.

Allioli (with fresh eggs)

1 large egg yolk, at room temperature

1 tbsp white wine vinegar or freshly squeezed lemon juice

2 large garlic cloves

10 tbsp Spanish olive oil

salt and pepper

Put the egg yolk, vinegar, garlic, and salt and pepper to taste in a food processor and blend together well.

With the motor running, very slowly add the oil, drop by drop at first, then, when it begins to thicken, in a slow, steady stream until the sauce is thick and smooth. Cover and chill in the refrigerator until ready to use.

Allioli (with bought mayonnaise)

4 tbsp store-bought mayonnaise

2 garlic cloves, crushed

4 tbsp Spanish extra virgin olive oil

1 tsp freshly squeezed lemon juice

Put the mayonnaise in a bowl and whisk until smooth. Add the garlic, then very slowly whisk in the oil, drop by drop, until it is all incorporated and the sauce is thick. Stir in the lemon juice. Cover and chill in the refrigerator until ready to use.

Variations
These variations are made by adding the ingredients at the end of preparing either of the preceding recipes.

Caper Allioli
Add 2 tablespoons of capers, finely chopped, and 1 tablespoon of chopped fresh parsley.

Green Allioli
Blanch 3 large spinach leaves quickly in boiling water, then drain and chop finely. Leave until cold, then add 1 tablespoon of chopped fresh parsley.

Herb Allioli
Add 2 tablespoons of chopped fresh parsley and 2 tablespoons of snipped chives.

Mustard Allioli
Add 1 tablespoon of whole-grain mustard.

Saffron Allioli
Put a pinch of saffron strands in a small bowl, then add 1 tablespoon of hot water and let soak for 10–15 minutes. Add the saffron liquid when cold.

Share and enjoy the tapas experience

The range and variety of tapas dishes to enjoy are enormous, and a selection of the best are to be found in this book. You don't have to sit in a bar to try these delicious small dishes. Tapas are for sharing, so select your favorite dishes and provide a bottle of your favorite drink. Cheers, or *salud*, as they say in Spanish!

Dips and Bread

Bread (*pan*) is the staple food of Spain and is served with every meal, so a tapa would hardly be complete without it. It is also bad manners in Spain not to eat everything on your plate, and so anyone who does not mop up their plate with their bread is considered badly educated!

Bread-based tapas can be prepared in advance, although if you prepare it too early the bread can become soft. Spanish bread is bought daily and eaten fresh, as it does not keep for long. Many are coarse-textured country-style loaves, so, for authenticity, choose something similar. A long, white loaf is also popular and not dissimilar to French bread, although the Spanish would say that it is better!

Catalan toasts

Catalán pa amb tomàquet

Serves 8 as part of a tapas meal

2 garlic cloves

2 large tomatoes

8 slices day-old French bread or small rounds country bread or sourdough bread, about 3/4 inch/2 cm thick

choice of toppings such as slices of serrano ham, slices of Manchego cheese, or pieces of roasted red bell pepper (optional)

3 tbsp Spanish extra virgin olive oil

pepper

Without doubt, this is the most ubiquitous, classic, and simplest tapa. It originates from Catalonia, where it is called "bread with tomatoes," but in the rest of Spain, it is simply known as Catalan Toast.

Preheat the broiler to high. Halve the garlic cloves. Coarsely grate the tomatoes into a bowl, discarding the skins left in your hand, and season to taste with pepper.

Toast the bread slices under the broiler until lightly golden brown on both sides. While the bread slices are still warm, rub with the cut side of the garlic halves to flavor, then top with the grated tomatoes. If using, add a slice of ham or Manchego cheese or a piece of roasted red bell pepper. Drizzle each with a little of the oil and serve immediately.

Chorizo bread pockets

Paquetitos empanados de chorizo

Makes 16

scant 1¹/₂ cups white bread flour,
plus extra for dusting

1¹/₂ tsp active dry yeast

¹/₂ tsp salt

¹/₄ tsp superfine sugar

¹/₂ cup warm water

sunflower-seed oil, for oiling

4 oz/115 g chorizo sausage,
outer casing removed

Allioli, to serve (optional)

Chorizo sausage, of which there are many varieties, is a favorite tapa ingredient. Often eaten with a slice of bread, it is encased here within a pocket of bread.

To make the bread dough, put the flour, yeast, salt, and sugar in a large bowl and make a well in the center. Pour the water into the well and gradually mix in the flour from the side. Using your hands, mix together to form a soft dough that leaves the side of the bowl clean.

Turn the dough onto a lightly floured counter and knead for 10 minutes, or until smooth and elastic and no longer sticky. Shape the dough into a ball and put in a clean bowl. Cover with a clean, damp dish towel and leave in a warm place for 1 hour, or until the dough has risen and doubled in size.

Preheat the oven to 400°F/200°C. Oil a cookie sheet. Cut the chorizo sausage into 16 equal-size chunks. Turn out the risen dough onto a lightly floured counter and knead lightly for 2–3 minutes to knock out the air.

Divide the dough into 16 equal-size pieces. Shape each piece into a ball and roll out on a lightly floured counter to a 4¹/₂-inch/12-cm circle. Put a piece of chorizo on each circle and gather the dough at the top, enclosing the chorizo, then pinch the edges together well to seal. Put each dough pocket, pinched-side down, on the prepared cookie sheet.

Bake in the preheated oven for 20 minutes, or until pale golden brown. Turn the pockets over so that the pinched ends are uppermost and arrange in a serving basket. Serve hot, as soon after baking as possible, because the pockets become dry on standing. Accompany with a bowl of Allioli for dipping, if using.

Cook's tip

As an alternative to making the bread dough, you could use half a 1 lb 2-oz/500-g package of white bread mix. Make up as directed on the package, remembering to use only half the quantity of water suggested.

Artichoke and pimiento flatbread

Pan campestre de alcachofa y pimienta

Makes 12 slices

4 tbsp Spanish olive oil, plus extra for oiling

2 large onions, thinly sliced

2 garlic cloves, finely chopped

14 oz/400 g canned artichoke hearts, drained and quartered

11¼ oz/320 g bottled or canned pimientos del piquillo, drained and thinly sliced

scant ¼ cup pitted black Spanish olives (optional)

salt and pepper

Bread dough

generous 2¾ cups white bread flour, plus extra for dusting

1½ tsp active dry yeast

1 tsp salt

½ tsp superfine sugar

¾ cup warm water

3 tbsp Spanish olive oil

This is the Spanish equivalent of the Italian pizza and, like the pizza, the toppings can vary enormously. The only difference is that Spanish flatbreads do not often contain cheese.

To make the bread dough, put the flour, yeast, salt, and sugar in a large bowl and make a well in the center. Mix the water and oil together in a pitcher and pour into the well, then gradually mix in the flour from the side. Using your hands, mix together to form a soft dough that leaves the side of the bowl clean.

Turn out the dough onto a lightly floured counter and knead for 10 minutes, or until smooth and elastic and no longer sticky. Shape the dough into a ball and put in a clean bowl. Cover with a clean, damp dish towel and leave in a warm place for 1 hour, or until the dough has risen and doubled in size.

Meanwhile, heat 3 tablespoons of the oil in a large skillet, then add the onions and cook over medium heat, stirring occasionally, for 10 minutes, or until golden brown. Add the garlic and cook, stirring, for 30 seconds, or until softened. Let cool. When cool, stir in the artichoke hearts and pimientos del piquillo, then season to taste with salt and pepper.

Preheat the oven to 400°F/200°C. Oil a large cookie sheet. Turn out the risen dough onto a lightly floured counter and knead lightly for 2–3 minutes to knock out the air. Roll out the dough to a 12-inch/30-cm square and transfer to the prepared cookie sheet.

Brush the remaining oil over the dough and spread the artichoke and pimiento mixture on top. Sprinkle over the olives, if using. Bake in the preheated oven for 20–25 minutes, or until golden brown and crisp. Cut into 12 slices and serve hot or warm.

Cook's tip

Pimientos del piquillo are long, sweet red peppers that have been roasted, peeled, and seeded. They are available in larger supermarkets in jars and cans, whole or sliced, and preserved in brine or oil.

Toast topped with asparagus and scrambled eggs

Huevos revueltos con espárrago y tostada

Serves 6 as part of a tapas meal

1 lb/450 g asparagus, trimmed and coarsely chopped

2 tbsp Spanish olive oil

1 onion, finely chopped

1 garlic clove, finely chopped

6 eggs

1 tbsp water

6 small slices country bread

salt and pepper

Scrambled eggs served with bread are popular in northern Spain. Apart from asparagus, recipes include chorizo sausage, mushrooms, tomatoes, bell peppers, and shrimp, or a combination of ingredients. You are limited only by your imagination!

Steam the asparagus pieces for 8 minutes or cook in a large pan of boiling salted water for 4 minutes, depending on their thickness, or until just tender. Drain well, if necessary.

Meanwhile, heat the oil in a large skillet, then add the onion and cook over medium heat, stirring occasionally, for 5 minutes, or until softened but not browned. Add the garlic and cook, stirring, for 30 seconds until softened.

Stir the asparagus into the skillet and cook, stirring occasionally, for 3–4 minutes. Meanwhile, break the eggs into a bowl, then add the water and beat together. Season to taste with salt and pepper.

Preheat the broiler to high. Add the beaten eggs to the asparagus mixture and cook, stirring constantly, for 2 minutes, or until the eggs have just set. Remove from the heat.

Toast the bread slices under the broiler until golden brown on both sides. Pile the scrambled eggs on top of the toast and serve immediately.

Cook's tip
Do not overcook the eggs; they should be just set, not firm, as they continue to cook when removed from the heat. A little chopped serrano ham, added with the garlic, is often included in this recipe.

Cheese and garlic dip with sun-dried tomato toasts

Tostadas de tomate seco con salsa de queso y ajo

Serves 6 as part of a tapas meal

8 oz/225 g soft goat cheese

2 tbsp Spanish extra virgin olive oil, plus extra for oiling

2 tsp freshly squeezed lemon juice

2 garlic cloves, crushed

1 tsp hot or sweet smoked Spanish paprika

generous 1/8 cup pitted green Spanish olives, finely chopped

1 tbsp chopped fresh flat-leaf parsley

Sun-dried tomato toasts

1 3/4 oz/50 g sun-dried tomatoes in oil, drained and 3 tbsp oil reserved

1 garlic clove, crushed

1 long French bread

There are numerous Spanish cheeses, but although some are becoming more widely available outside Spain, many are not produced on a large enough scale to be exported. Fortunately, any soft variety of goat cheese can be used in this recipe.

Preheat the oven to 400°F/200°C. Generously oil a cookie sheet. To make the toasts, very finely chop the tomatoes and put in a bowl. Add the reserved oil from the tomatoes and garlic and mix together well.

Slice the bread into 1/2-inch/1-cm thick slices and spread with the tomato mixture. Put on the prepared cookie sheet and bake in the preheated oven for 10 minutes, or until golden brown and crisp. Let cool on a cooling rack.

To make the dip, put the goat cheese in a food processor. With the motor running, add 1 tablespoon of the oil, drop by drop. Using a spatula, scrape down the side of the bowl. With the motor running again, very slowly add the remaining oil and the lemon juice in a thin, steady stream. Add the garlic and paprika and process until well mixed.

Stir the olives and parsley into the dip. Turn the dip into a small serving bowl, then cover and chill in the refrigerator for at least 1 hour before serving.

Serve the dip accompanied by the toasts.

Variation

Instead of using olives, the same quantity of capers or gherkins could be added to the dip.

Wild mushroom and allioli toasts

Tostada de setas y allioli

Makes 10

5 tbsp Spanish olive oil

2 large garlic cloves, finely chopped

1 lb/450 g wild, exotic, or cultivated
mushrooms, sliced

2 tbsp dry Spanish sherry

4 tbsp chopped fresh
flat-leaf parsley

10 slices long, thick crusty bread

8 tbsp Allioli

salt and pepper

Wild mushrooms, as suggested in this recipe, should be picked and gathered
by experienced mushroom hunters only. Should you find these difficult to buy,
exotic or cultivated mushrooms can be used as a substitute.

Heat the oil in a large skillet, then add the garlic and cook over medium heat, stirring, for 30 seconds, or until softened. Increase the heat to high, then add the mushrooms and cook, stirring constantly, until the mushrooms are coated in the oil and all the oil has been absorbed.

Reduce the heat to low and cook for 2–3 minutes, or until all the juices have been released from the mushrooms. Add the sherry, increase the heat to high again and cook, stirring frequently, for 3–4 minutes until the liquid has evaporated. Stir in the parsley and season to taste with salt and pepper.

Meanwhile, preheat the broiler to high. Toast the bread slices under the broiler until lightly golden brown on both sides.

Spread the Allioli on top of each toast and top with the cooked mushrooms. Carefully transfer the toasts to a broiler rack and cook under the broiler until the Allioli starts to bubble. Serve hot.

Cook's tip
Eggplants and zucchini can be cooked in the same way as these mushrooms, first over high heat and then over low heat.

Roman dip with anchovy circles

Garum con rondallas de anchoa

Serves 12 as part of a tapas meal

1 egg

scant 1 cup pitted black
Spanish olives

1³/4 oz/50 g canned anchovy fillets
in olive oil, drained and oil set aside

2 garlic cloves, 1 crushed and
1 peeled but kept whole

1 tbsp capers

¹/2 tsp hot or sweet smoked
Spanish paprika

1 tbsp Spanish brandy or sherry

4 tbsp Spanish extra virgin olive oil

1 small French bread

pepper

This black olive dip, introduced to Spain by the Romans (hence its name), is Spain's version of the French tapenade. Made with olives, anchovies, capers, garlic, and olive oil, the ingredients capture the essential flavor of Spanish cooking.

Put the egg in a pan, then cover with cold water and slowly bring to a boil. Reduce the heat and simmer gently for 10 minutes. Immediately drain the egg and rinse under cold running water to cool. Gently tap the egg to crack the shell and leave until cold.

When the egg is cold, crack the shell all over and remove it. Put the egg in a food processor and add the olives, 2 of the anchovy fillets, the crushed garlic, capers, paprika, and brandy and process to a coarse paste. With the motor running, very slowly add 1 tablespoon of the reserved oil from the anchovies and the extra virgin olive oil in a thin, steady stream. Season the dip to taste with pepper.

Turn the dip into a small serving bowl, then cover and chill in the refrigerator until ready to serve.

To make the anchovy circles, put the remaining anchovy fillets, remaining reserved oil from the anchovies, and garlic clove in a mortar and, using a pestle, pound together to a paste. Turn the paste into a bowl, then cover and chill in the refrigerator until ready to serve.

When ready to serve, preheat the broiler to high. Slice the French bread into 1-inch/2.5-cm circles and toast under the broiler until golden brown on both sides. Spread the anchovy paste very thinly on the toasted bread circles and serve with the dip.

Cook's tip
As well as serving this as a dip, it can also be used, as the Romans did, to flavor dishes such as meatballs and salad dressings. You can also use green olives instead of the black olives, or a mixture of black and green olives.

Roasted red bell peppers on garlic toasts

Escalibada con tostada y ajo

Makes 8

4 thin slices white country bread
5 tbsp Spanish olive oil
2 large garlic cloves, crushed
3 large red bell peppers
pepper
chopped fresh flat-leaf parsley,
to garnish

Escalibada is a Catalan specialty and refers to the roasting of eggplants or bell peppers. In this recipe, the peppers are roasted in an oven in the traditional way, but although referred to as roasted peppers, they are often broiled or grilled.

Preheat the oven to 450°F/230°C. To make the garlic toasts, halve each bread slice. Put 3 tablespoons of the oil in a bowl and stir in the garlic. Brush each side of the bread slice halves with the oil mixture and transfer to a cookie sheet. Bake in the preheated oven for 10–15 minutes, or until crisp and golden brown. Let cool on paper towels.

Reduce the oven temperature to 400°F/200°C. Brush the red bell peppers with the remaining oil and put in a roasting pan. Roast in the oven for 30 minutes, then turn over and roast for an additional 10 minutes, or until the skins have blistered and blackened.

Using a slotted spoon, transfer the roasted peppers to a plastic bag and leave for 15 minutes, or until cool enough to handle.

Using a sharp knife or your fingers, carefully peel away the skin from the peppers. Halve the bell peppers and remove the stems, cores, and seeds, then cut each bell pepper into neat, thin strips.

To serve, arrange the bell pepper strips on top of the garlic toasts. Season to taste with pepper and sprinkle with chopped parsley to garnish.

Cook's tip
This recipe uses red bell peppers, but it can be prepared with yellow or green bell peppers if preferred. If you are short of time, jars of roasted, peeled red bell peppers are available and can be found in most large supermarkets.

Fresh mint and bean pâté

Pâté de haba gruesa con menta

Serves 12 as part of a tapas meal

1 lb 12 oz/800 g fresh fava beans in their pods, shelled to give about 12 oz/350 g

8 oz/225 g soft goat cheese

1 garlic clove, crushed

2 scallions, finely chopped

1 tbsp Spanish extra virgin olive oil, plus extra to serve

grated rind and 2 tbsp lemon juice

about 60 large fresh mint leaves, about ½ oz/15 g in total

12 slices French bread

salt and pepper

Pâtés are usually associated with meat, but this is a vegetable pâté combining fava beans and cheese with the fresh taste of mint. Pâtés are, of course, of French origin, but have now found their way to the tapas bars of Spain.

Cook the fava beans in a pan of boiling water for 8–10 minutes, or until tender. Drain well and let cool. When the beans are cool enough to handle, slip off their skins and put the beans in a food processor. This is a laborious task, but worth doing if you have the time. This quantity will take about 15 minutes to skin.

Add the goat cheese, garlic, scallions, oil, lemon rind and juice, and mint leaves to the fava beans and process until well mixed. Season the pâté to taste with salt and pepper. Turn into a bowl, cover then chill in the refrigerator for at least 1 hour before serving.

To serve, preheat the broiler to high. Toast the bread slices under the broiler until golden brown on both sides. Drizzle a little oil over the toasted bread slices, then spread the pâté on top and serve immediately.

Cook's tip

If fresh fava beans are not available or it is more convenient, you can use frozen baby fava beans instead. You will need 12 oz/350 g and they should be cooked for 4–5 minutes, or until tender.

Meat and Poultry

Apart from in the north and parts of central Spain, good pasture land is scarce and therefore cattle have not been traditionally raised for meat or dairy produce. This means that there are far more Spanish recipes for pork than there are for beef. Cured Spanish ham is even eaten in larger quantities than fresh pork, as is cooked ham. Fresh pork is also used to make Spanish sausages such as chorizo.

Sheep, however, are raised in the western and central grazing regions and the eastern mountainous areas of Spain, and fine lamb is also produced. Chicken, too, is very popular in Spain and several classic tapas dishes are included in this chapter.

Sautéed chicken with crispy garlic slices

Pollo con ajo

Serves 8 as part of a tapas meal

8 skin-on chicken thighs, boned if available

hot or sweet smoked Spanish paprika, to taste

4 tbsp Spanish olive oil

10 garlic cloves, sliced

1/2 cup dry white wine

1 bay leaf

salt

chopped fresh flat-leaf parsley, to garnish

crusty bread, to serve (optional)

This classic Spanish recipe can be found in most Spanish restaurants, but when the chicken is cut into bite-size pieces rather than larger portions, it is ideal to serve as a tapa.

If necessary, halve the chicken thighs and remove the bones, then cut the flesh into bite-size pieces, leaving the skin on. Season to taste with paprika.

Heat the oil in a large skillet or an ovenproof casserole, then add the garlic slices and cook over medium heat, stirring frequently, for 1 minute, or until golden brown. Remove with a slotted spoon and drain on paper towels.

Add the chicken thighs to the skillet and cook, turning occasionally, for 10 minutes, or until tender and golden brown on all sides. Add the wine and bay leaf and bring to a boil. Reduce the heat and simmer, stirring occasionally, for 10 minutes, or until most of the liquid has evaporated and the juices run clear when a skewer is inserted into the thickest part of the meat. Season to taste with salt.

Transfer the chicken to a warmed serving dish and sprinkle over the reserved garlic slices. Sprinkle with chopped parsley to garnish and serve with chunks of crusty bread to mop up the juices, if using.

Variation
This dish is equally good when made with turkey or rabbit instead of the chicken. You could also use dry sherry instead of the wine.

Chicken, raisin, and pine nut salad

Ensalada de pollo con pasitas y piñones

Serves 6–8 as part of a tapas meal

¼ cup red wine vinegar

⅛ cup superfine sugar

1 bay leaf

pared rind of 1 lemon

scant 1 cup seedless raisins

4 large skinless, boneless chicken breasts, about 1 lb 5 oz/600 g in total

5 tbsp Spanish olive oil

1 garlic clove, finely chopped

1 cup pine nuts

generous ⅓ cup Spanish extra virgin olive oil

1 small bunch of fresh flat-leaf parsley, finely chopped

salt and pepper

The combination of raisins and pine nuts has been used in Spanish, Italian, and Middle Eastern cooking for centuries, but which country the combination originated in is uncertain. Whoever created it, the result is delicious!

To make the dressing, put the vinegar, sugar, bay leaf, and lemon rind in a pan and bring to a boil, then remove from the heat. Stir in the raisins and let cool.

When the dressing is cool, slice the chicken breasts widthwise into very thin slices. Heat the olive oil in a large skillet, then add the chicken slices and cook over medium heat, stirring occasionally, for 8–10 minutes, or until lightly browned and tender.

Add the garlic and pine nuts and cook, stirring constantly and shaking the skillet, for 1 minute, or until the pine nuts are golden brown. Season to taste with salt and pepper.

Pour the cooled dressing into a large bowl, discarding the bay leaf and lemon rind. Add the extra virgin olive oil and whisk together. Season to taste with salt and pepper. Add the chicken mixture and parsley and toss together. Turn the salad into a serving dish and serve warm or, if serving cold, cover and chill in the refrigerator for 2–3 hours before serving.

Cook's tip
For an authentic touch, use seedless, sweet Malaga muscatel raisins, available from some health food stores.

Spicy Moroccan chicken kabobs

Pinchos moruños

Serves 4 as part of a tapas meal

1 lb/450 g chicken breast fillets

3 tbsp Spanish olive oil, plus extra
for oiling

juice of 1 lemon

2 garlic cloves, crushed

1¹/2 tsp ground cumin

1 tsp ground coriander

1 tsp hot or sweet smoked
Spanish paprika

¹/4 tsp ground cinnamon

¹/2 tsp dried oregano

salt

chopped fresh flat-leaf parsley,
to garnish

Pinchos are marinated kabobs of Moroccan origin and use a blend of spices to flavor them. As this blend may be difficult to obtain, this recipe uses a combination of spices that are not dissimilar.

Cut the chicken into 1-inch/2.5-cm cubes and put in a large, shallow, nonreactive dish. Put all the remaining ingredients, except the parsley to garnish, in a bowl and whisk together. Pour the marinade over the chicken cubes and toss the meat in the marinade until well coated. Cover and let marinate in the refrigerator for 8 hours or overnight, turning the chicken 2–3 times if possible.

If using wooden skewers or toothpicks, soak the skewers in cold water for about 30 minutes to help prevent them from burning and the food sticking to them during cooking. If using metal skewers, preferably flat ones, lightly brush with oil.

Preheat the broiler, griddle, or barbecue. Remove the chicken pieces from the marinade, reserving the remaining marinade, and thread an equal quantity onto each prepared skewer or toothpick, leaving a little space between each piece.

Brush the broiler rack or griddle with a little oil. Add the kabobs and cook, turning frequently and brushing with the reserved marinade halfway through cooking, for 15 minutes, or until browned on all sides, tender, and cooked through. Serve hot, sprinkled with chopped parsley to garnish.

Variation

In Morocco, pinchos are prepared with lamb and in Spain they are usually prepared with pork, and either of these meats could be used to replace the chicken in this recipe.

Spanish meatballs with cracked olives

Albóndigas con aceitunas abiertas

Serves 6 as part of a tapas meal

2 oz/55 g day-old bread, crusts removed

3 tbsp water

1⅛ cups lean fresh ground pork

1⅛ cups lean fresh ground lamb

2 small onions, finely chopped

3 garlic cloves, crushed

1 tsp ground cumin

1 tsp ground coriander

1 egg, lightly beaten

all-purpose flour, for dusting

3 tbsp Spanish olive oil

14 oz/400 g canned chopped tomatoes

5 tbsp dry sherry or red wine

pinch of hot or sweet smoked Spanish paprika

pinch of sugar

1 cup cracked green olives in extra virgin olive oil

salt

crusty bread, to serve

Meatballs are one of the most popular tapas dishes. Ground pork and lamb are the usual combination used to make these meatballs in Spain, but there is no reason why you could not use pork and beef or veal, or any of these meats on their own.

Put the bread in a bowl, then add the water and let soak for 30 minutes. Using your hands, squeeze out as much of the water as possible from the bread and put the bread in a clean bowl.

Add the ground meat, 1 chopped onion, 2 crushed garlic cloves, the cumin, coriander, and egg to the bread. Season to taste with salt and, using your hands, mix together well. Dust a plate or cookie sheet with flour. Using floured hands, roll the mixture into 30 equal-size, small balls, then put on the plate or cookie sheet and roll lightly in the flour.

Heat 2 tablespoons of the oil in a large skillet, then add the meatballs, in batches to avoid overcrowding, and cook over medium heat, turning frequently, for 8–10 minutes, until golden brown on all sides and firm. Remove with a slotted spoon and set aside.

Heat the remaining oil in the skillet, then add the remaining onion and cook, stirring occasionally, for 5 minutes, or until softened but not browned. Add the remaining garlic and cook, stirring, for 30 seconds. Add the tomatoes and their juice, sherry, paprika, and sugar and season to taste with salt. Bring to a boil, then reduce the heat and simmer for 10 minutes.

Using a hand-held blender, blend the tomato mixture until smooth. Alternatively, turn the tomato mixture into a food processor or blender and process until smooth. Return the sauce to the pan.

Carefully return the meatballs to the skillet and add the olives. Simmer gently for 20 minutes, or until the meatballs are tender. Serve hot, with crusty bread to mop up the sauce.

Cook's tip
Cracked green olives are made by cracking unripe green olives and putting them in water for several weeks to remove their bitterness, then storing them in brine. If you are unable to find these, green olives in extra virgin olive oil could be used instead.

Spareribs coated in paprika sauce

Costillas adobadas de pimentón

Paprika is used to season dishes in Spain in the same way that other countries use pepper. Made from a small dried red pepper, there are several varieties available; in this recipe you can use whichever type you prefer.

Serves 6 as part of a tapas meal

olive oil, for oiling

2 lb 12 oz/1.25 kg pork spareribs

generous 1/3 cup dry Spanish sherry

5 tsp hot or sweet smoked Spanish paprika

2 garlic cloves, crushed

1 tbsp dried oregano

2/3 cup water

salt

Preheat the oven to 425°F/220°C. Oil a large roasting pan. If the butcher has not already done so, cut the sheets of spareribs into individual ribs. If possible, cut each sparerib in half widthwise. Put the spareribs in the prepared pan, in a single layer, and roast in the preheated oven for 20 minutes.

Meanwhile, make the sauce. Put the sherry, paprika, garlic, oregano, water, and salt to taste in a pitcher and mix together well.

Reduce the oven temperature to 350°F/180°C. Pour off the fat from the pan, then pour the sauce over the spareribs and turn the spareribs to coat with the sauce on both sides. Roast for an additional 45 minutes, basting the spareribs with the sauce once halfway through the cooking time, until tender.

Pile the spareribs into a warmed serving dish. Bring the sauce in the roasting pan to a boil on the stove, then reduce the heat and simmer until reduced by half. Pour the sauce over the spareribs and serve hot.

Cook's tip
Provide plenty of napkins and finger bowls when serving the spareribs for wiping fingers.

Spanish mountain ham croquettes

Croquetas de jamón serrano

Makes 8

4 tbsp Spanish olive oil

1 small onion, finely chopped

1 garlic clove, crushed

4 tbsp all-purpose flour

scant 1 cup milk

7 oz/200 g Serrano ham or cooked ham, in one piece, finely diced

pinch of hot or sweet smoked Spanish paprika

1 egg

1 cup day-old white breadcrumbs

sunflower-seed oil, for deep-frying

salt

Allioli, to serve

Clever Spanish cooks avoid wasting anything, and to make this recipe they use up the last of the piece of *jamón serrano* (mountain ham) that they were given for Christmas. However, you can use any air-cured or cooked ham.

Heat the olive oil in a pan, then add the onion and cook over medium heat, stirring occasionally, for 5 minutes, or until softened but not browned. Add the garlic and cook, stirring, for 30 seconds. Stir in the flour and cook over low heat, stirring constantly, for 1 minute without the mixture coloring.

Remove the pan from the heat and gradually stir in the milk to form a smooth sauce. Return to the heat and slowly bring to a boil, stirring constantly, until the sauce boils and thickens.

Remove the pan from the heat, then stir in the ham and paprika and season to taste with salt. Spread the mixture in a shallow dish and let cool, then cover and chill in the refrigerator for at least 2 hours or overnight.

When the mixture has chilled, break the egg onto a plate and beat lightly. Spread the breadcrumbs on a separate plate. Using wet hands, form the ham mixture into 8 even-size pieces and form each piece into a cylindrical shape. Dip the croquettes, one at a time, into the beaten egg, then roll in the breadcrumbs to coat. Put on a plate and chill in the refrigerator for at least 1 hour.

Heat enough sunflower-seed oil for deep-frying in a deep-fat fryer to 350–375°F/180–190°C, or until a cube of bread browns in 30 seconds. Add the croquettes, in batches to avoid overcrowding, and cook for 5 minutes, or until golden brown and crisp. Remove with a slotted spoon or draining basket and drain on paper towels. Keep hot in a warm oven while you cook the remaining croquettes. Serve hot with Allioli.

Ham and goat cheese empanadillas

Empanadillas de jamón y queso de cabra

Makes about 32

1 tbsp olive oil

1 small onion, finely chopped

1 garlic clove, crushed

5¹/₂ oz/150 g soft goat cheese

6 oz/175 g thickly sliced cooked ham, finely chopped

scant ¹/₂ cup capers, chopped

¹/₂ tsp hot or sweet smoked Spanish paprika

1 lb 2 oz/500 g ready-made puff pastry, thawed if frozen

beaten egg, to glaze

all-purpose flour, for dusting

salt

Literally translated, *empanadilla* means "covered in bread," but the usual covering is pie dough, which is then deep-fried or baked. Circles of pie dough can be bought in Spain, but for ease this recipe uses ready-made puff pastry, which is then baked.

Preheat the oven to 400°F/200°C. Dampen several large cookie sheets. Heat the oil in a large skillet, then add the onion and cook over medium heat, stirring occasionally, for 5 minutes, or until softened but not browned. Add the garlic and cook, stirring, for 30 seconds.

Put the goat cheese in a bowl, then add the ham, capers, onion mixture, and paprika and mix together well. Season to taste with salt.

Thinly roll out the pastry on a lightly floured counter. Using a plain, 3¹/₄-inch/8-cm round cutter, cut out 32 circles, rerolling the trimmings as necessary.

Using a teaspoon, put an equal, small amount of the goat cheese mixture in the center of each pastry circle. Dampen the edges of the pastry with a little water and fold one half over the other to form a crescent and enclose the filling. Pinch the edges together with your fingers to seal, then press with the tines of a fork to seal further. Transfer to the prepared cookie sheets.

With the tip of a sharp knife, make a small slit in the top of each pastry and brush with beaten egg to glaze. Bake in the preheated oven for 15 minutes, or until risen and golden brown. Serve warm.

Chorizo and fava bean tortilla

Tortilla de chorizo y habas

Serves 8 as part of a tapas meal

8 oz/225 g frozen baby
fava beans

6 eggs

3 1/2 oz/100 g chorizo sausage,
outer casing removed, chopped

3 tbsp Spanish olive oil

1 onion, chopped

salt and pepper

The tortilla, or Spanish omelet, is a firm, thick, set cake, unlike the French soft-set omelet. The classic recipe contains just potatoes, eggs, and onion, but other vegetables are often used and fava beans and chorizo sausage are very good.

Cook the fava beans in a pan of boiling water for 4 minutes. Drain well and let cool. Meanwhile, lightly beat the eggs in a large bowl. Add the chorizo sausage and season to taste with salt and pepper.

When the beans are cool enough to handle, slip off their skins. This is a laborious task, but worth doing if you have the time. This quantity will take about 15 minutes to skin.

Heat the oil in a large skillet, then add the onion and cook over medium heat, stirring occasionally, for 5 minutes, or until softened but not browned. Add the fava beans and cook, stirring, for 1 minute.

Pour the egg mixture into the skillet and cook gently for 2–3 minutes, or until the underside is just set and lightly browned. Use a spatula to loosen the tortilla away from the side and bottom of the skillet to let the uncooked egg run underneath and prevent the tortilla from sticking to the bottom.

Cover the tortilla with a large, upside-down plate and invert the tortilla onto it. Slide the tortilla back into the skillet, cooked-side up, and cook for an additional 2–3 minutes, or until the underside is lightly browned.

Slide the tortilla onto a warmed serving dish. Serve warm, cut into small cubes.

Sirloin steak with garlic and sherry

Solomillo con ajo y jerez

Serves 6–8 as part of a tapas meal

4 sirloin steaks, about
6–8 oz/175–225 g each and
1 inch/2.5 cm thick

5 garlic cloves

3 tbsp Spanish olive oil

½ cup dry Spanish sherry

salt and pepper

chopped fresh flat-leaf parsley,
to garnish

crusty bread, to serve

Beef does not feature in many tapas recipes, but fortunately this dish of tender bite-size morsels of steak, in a garlic and sherry sauce, is not one that you will tire of!

Cut the steaks into 1-inch/2.5-cm cubes and put in a large, shallow dish. Slice 3 of the garlic cloves and set aside. Finely chop the remaining garlic cloves and sprinkle over the steak cubes. Season generously with pepper and mix together well. Cover and let marinate in the refrigerator for 1–2 hours.

Heat the oil in a large skillet, then add the garlic slices and cook over low heat, stirring, for 1 minute, or until golden brown. Increase the heat to medium–high, then add the steak cubes and cook, stirring constantly, for 2–3 minutes, or until browned and almost cooked to your liking.

Add the sherry and cook until it has evaporated slightly. Season to taste with salt and turn into a warmed serving dish. Garnish with chopped parsley and serve hot, accompanied by chunks or slices of crusty bread to mop up the juices.

Cook's tip

Provide toothpicks to spear the pieces of steak for eating.

Calves' liver in almond saffron sauce

Hígado de ternero en salsa de azafrán y almendras

Serves 6 as part of a tapas meal

4 tbsp Spanish olive oil

1 oz/25 g white bread

2/3 cup blanched almonds

2 garlic cloves, crushed

pinch of saffron strands

2/3 cup dry Spanish sherry
or white wine

1¼ cups vegetable stock

1 lb/450 g calves' liver

all-purpose flour, for dusting

salt and pepper

chopped fresh flat-leaf parsley,
to garnish

crusty bread, to serve

Almonds and saffron are both ingredients that were introduced to Spanish cuisine when the country was inhabited by the Moors. One of the classic tapas dishes is meatballs in almond saffron sauce, but here, tender calves' liver is used.

To make the sauce, heat 2 tablespoons of the oil in a large skillet. Tear the bread into small pieces and add to the skillet with the almonds. Cook over low heat, stirring frequently, for 2 minutes, or until golden brown. Stir in the garlic and cook, stirring, for 30 seconds.

Add the saffron and sherry to the skillet and season to taste with salt and pepper. Bring to a boil and continue to boil for 1–2 minutes. Remove from the heat and let cool slightly, then transfer the mixture to a food processor. Add the stock and process until smooth. Set aside.

Cut the liver into large bite-size pieces. Dust lightly with flour and season generously with pepper. Heat the remaining oil in the skillet, then add the liver and cook over medium heat, stirring constantly, for 2–3 minutes, or until firm and lightly browned.

Pour the sauce into the skillet and reheat gently for 1–2 minutes. Transfer to a warmed serving dish and garnish with chopped parsley. Serve hot, accompanied by chunks of crusty bread to mop up the sauce.

Variation
Lambs' liver, chicken livers, or lambs' kidneys can all be prepared in the same way as the calves' liver.

Fish and Seafood

The Mediterranean Sea and the Atlantic Ocean lap Spain's long coastline, providing a wealth of sea fish and shellfish, and in Spain's fast-flowing rivers and mountain streams, freshwater fish are caught in abundance. It is true to say that fish is Spain's favorite, most frequently eaten food, and this is reflected by the choice of delicious dishes.

A selection of tapas would not be complete without a shellfish dish, and this is particularly true in the south, which is famous for its fried fish. Shrimp are the shellfish that usually find their way onto a tapas menu, either simply broiled or fried and eaten with your fingers or in a sauce, as in the recipe here for Tossed shrimp and bell peppers in garlic sauce.

Mixed seafood kabobs with a chili and lime glaze

Pinchitos de mariscos glaseados con pimentón y lima

Makes 8

16 raw jumbo shrimp, in their shells

12 oz/350 g angler fish or hake fillet

12 oz/350 g salmon fillet, skinned

1-inch/2.5-cm piece fresh gingerroot

4 tbsp sweet chili sauce

grated rind and juice of 1 lime

sunflower-seed or olive oil, for oiling (optional)

lime wedges, to serve

A mixture of fish and shellfish is ideal for threading onto skewers, and although these are cooked under a conventional broiler, they are equally delicious cooked over a grill.

Pull off the heads of the shrimp. With your fingers, peel away the shells, leaving the tails intact. Using a sharp knife, make a shallow slit along the underside of each shrimp, then use the tip of the knife to lift out the dark vein and discard. Rinse the shrimp under cold running water and pat dry with paper towels. Cut the angler fish and salmon into 1-inch/2.5-cm pieces.

Grate the ginger into a strainer set over a large, nonreactive bowl to catch the juice. Squeeze the grated ginger to extract all the juice and discard the pulp.

Add the chili sauce and lime rind and juice to the ginger juice and mix together. Add the prepared seafood and stir to coat in the marinade. Cover and let marinate in the refrigerator for 30 minutes.

Meanwhile, if using wooden skewers, soak 8 in cold water for about 30 minutes to help prevent them from burning and the food sticking to them during cooking. If using metal skewers, preferably flat ones, lightly brush with oil.

Preheat the broiler to high and line the broiler pan with foil. Remove the seafood from the marinade, reserving the remaining marinade, and thread an equal quantity onto each prepared skewer, leaving a little space between each piece. Arrange in the broiler pan.

Cook the skewers under the broiler, turning once and brushing with the reserved marinade, for 6–8 minutes, or until cooked through. Serve hot, drizzled with the marinade in the broiler pan and with lime wedges for squeezing over.

Cook's tip

You could use angler fish tail instead of fillet, but buy about 3 oz/85 g extra to allow for the bone. Cut either side of the central bone with a sharp knife, discarding any membrane, and remove the flesh to form 2 fillets. Other fish could be used, but it is important that its flesh is firm. Cod and swordfish would be good choices.

Batter-fried fish sticks

Bastonetes fritos de pescado

Serves 6 as part of a tapas meal

generous 3/4 cup all-purpose flour, plus extra for dusting

pinch of salt

1 egg, beaten

1 tbsp Spanish olive oil

2/3 cup water

1 lb 5 oz/600 g firm-fleshed white fish fillet, such as angler fish or hake

sunflower-seed or olive oil, for deep-frying

lemon wedges, to serve

Batter-fried foods, known as *rebozados*, are particularly popular in tapas bars and may include vegetables, meat, or fish. The latter is often the most popular, especially in Spanish coastal areas.

To make the batter, put the flour and salt into a large bowl and make a well in the center. Pour the egg and olive oil into the well, then gradually add the water, mixing in the flour from the side and beating constantly, until all the flour is incorporated and a smooth batter forms.

Cut the fish into fingers about 3/4 inch/2 cm wide and 2 inches/5 cm long. Dust lightly with flour so that the batter sticks to them when dipped in it.

Heat enough sunflower-seed or olive oil for deep-frying in a deep-fat fryer to 350–375°F/ 180–190°C, or until a cube of bread browns in 30 seconds. Spear a fish stick onto a toothpick and dip into the batter, then drop the fish and toothpick into the hot oil. Cook the fish sticks, in batches to avoid overcrowding, for 5 minutes, or until golden brown. Remove with a slotted spoon or draining basket and drain on paper towels. Keep hot in a warm oven while cooking the remaining fish sticks.

Serve the fish sticks hot, with lemon wedges for squeezing over.

Cook's tip
If you wish to batter-fry other fish, try shrimp, scallops, cubes of fresh cod, or cubes of soaked salt cod.

Tuna and olive empanadillas

Empanadillas de atún con aceitunas

Makes about 32

6 oz/175 g canned tuna in olive oil

1 small onion, finely chopped

1 garlic clove, finely chopped

1³/₄ oz/50 g pimiento-stuffed Spanish olives, finely chopped

generous ¹/₈ cup pine nuts

1 lb 2 oz/500 g ready-made puff pastry, thawed if frozen

all-purpose flour, for dusting

beaten egg, to glaze

salt and pepper

Empanadillas are small pastries with a variety of fillings, which are pocket-size versions of *empanadas*, pies that originated in Spain's north-west region of Galicia. Tuna and vegetable fillings are particularly popular.

Drain the tuna, reserving the oil, put in a large bowl, and set aside. Heat 1 tablespoon of the reserved oil from the tuna in a large skillet, then add the onion and cook over medium heat, stirring occasionally, for 5 minutes, or until softened but not browned. Add the garlic and cook, stirring, for 30 seconds, or until softened.

Mash the tuna with a fork, then add the onion mixture, olives, and pine nuts and mix together well. Season to taste with salt and pepper.

Preheat the oven to 400°F/200°C. Dampen several large cookie sheets. Thinly roll out the pastry on a lightly floured counter. Using a plain, 3¹/₄-inch/8-cm round cutter, cut out 32 circles, rerolling the trimmings as necessary.

Using a teaspoon, put an equal, small amount of the tuna mixture in the center of each pastry circle. Dampen the edges of the pastry with a little water and fold one half over the other to form a crescent and enclose the filling. Pinch the edges together with your fingers to seal, then press with the tines of a fork to seal further. Transfer to the prepared cookie sheets.

With the tip of a sharp knife, make a small slit in the top of each pastry and brush with beaten egg to glaze. Bake in the preheated oven for 15 minutes, or until risen and golden brown. Serve warm.

Seared squid and golden potatoes

Calamar abrasado con patatas doradas

Serves 8 as part of a tapas meal

2 lb 4 oz/1 kg new potatoes

4–6 tbsp Spanish olive oil

1 large onion, thinly sliced

2 garlic cloves, finely chopped

2 lb 4 oz/1 kg cleaned squid bodies, thinly sliced

6 tbsp dry white wine

1 small bunch of fresh flat-leaf parsley, finely chopped

salt and pepper

lemon wedges, to serve

Preparing squid can be time-consuming, but fortunately it is possible to buy skinned and cleaned squid from fish suppliers and supermarkets. Squid and potatoes are a traditional Spanish combination.

Put the potatoes in a pan of water and bring to a boil. Reduce the heat and simmer for 20 minutes, or until tender. Drain well.

Heat 4 tablespoons of oil in a large ovenproof casserole, then add the potatoes and cook over medium heat, stirring occasionally, for 10 minutes, or until beginning to turn brown. Add the onion and cook, stirring occasionally, for 10 minutes, or until golden brown. Add the garlic and cook, stirring, for 30 seconds until softened. Push all the ingredients to the side of the casserole.

If necessary, add the remaining oil to the casserole. Add the squid slices and cook over high heat, stirring occasionally, for 2 minutes, or until golden brown. Add the wine and cook for an additional 1–2 minutes. Add most of the parsley, reserving a little to garnish, and mix the potatoes, onions, and garlic with the squid. Season to taste with salt and pepper.

Serve hot, in the casserole, sprinkled with the reserved parsley to garnish and with lemon wedges for squeezing over.

Cook's tip

To prepare the squid yourself, hold the body in one hand and pull on the head and tentacles with the other, which will bring the body contents away, too, to be discarded. Cut off the edible tentacles just above the eyes and set aside. Carefully remove the ink sacs from the head and set aside for another dish, if you wish. Discard the head. Remove the transparent quill and rub off the thin, dark outer membrane.

Tossed shrimp and bell peppers in garlic sauce

Gambas y pimientas en salsa de ajo

Serves 8 as part of a tapas meal

1 lb 2 oz/500 g raw jumbo shrimp, in their shells

2 tbsp Spanish olive oil

2 red bell peppers, cored, seeded, and thinly sliced

5 garlic cloves, finely chopped

juice of 1/2 lemon

6 tbsp dry Spanish sherry

salt and pepper

crusty bread, to serve

Shrimp are a hugely popular tapas dish, from simple fried shrimp to a more elaborate dish such as this one, and garlic is usually somewhere in evidence!

Pull off the heads of the shrimp. With your fingers, peel away the shells, leaving the tails intact. Using a sharp knife, make a shallow slit along the underside of each shrimp, then use the tip of the knife to lift out the dark vein and discard. Rinse the shrimp under cold running water and pat dry with paper towels.

Heat the oil in a large skillet, then add the red bell pepper slices and cook for 10–15 minutes, or until softened. Add the garlic and cook, stirring, for 30 seconds until softened.

Add the shrimp to the skillet and cook, tossing constantly, for 1–2 minutes, or until the shrimp turn pink. Add the lemon juice and sherry and cook for an additional 2 minutes, or until the shrimp begin to curl. Season to taste with salt and pepper.

Serve hot, with chunks or slices of crusty bread to mop up the garlic sauce.

Cook's tip

If more convenient, you could use shelled shrimp for this dish or frozen shrimp, but if you choose to use the latter, dry them thoroughly with paper towels once thawed.

Mussels in a vinaigrette dressing

Mejillones a la vinagreta

Serves 6 as part of a tapas meal

6 tbsp Spanish extra virgin olive oil

2 tbsp white wine vinegar

1 shallot, finely chopped

1 garlic clove, crushed

2 tbsp capers, chopped

1 fresh red chile, seeded and finely chopped (optional)

2 lb 4 oz/1 kg live mussels, in their shells

6 tbsp dry white wine

4 tbsp chopped fresh flat-leaf parsley

salt and pepper

crusty bread, to serve (optional)

Mussels can be prepared in numerous ways, but this is perhaps one of the simplest ways of serving them. The other advantage is that they can be prepared in advance.

To make the dressing, put the oil and vinegar in a bowl and whisk together. Stir in the shallot, garlic, capers, and chile, if using. Season to taste with salt and pepper.

Clean the mussels by scrubbing or scraping the shells and pulling out any beards that are attached to them. Discard any with broken shells or any that refuse to close when tapped. Put the mussels in a colander and rinse well under cold running water.

Put the mussels in a large pan and add the wine. Bring to a boil, then cover and cook over high heat, shaking the pan occasionally, for 3–4 minutes, or until the mussels have opened. Drain the mussels, discarding any that remain closed, and let cool.

When the mussels are cool enough to handle, discard the empty half shells and arrange the mussels, in their other half shells, in a large, shallow serving dish. Whisk the dressing again and spoon over the mussels. Cover and chill in the refrigerator for at least 1 hour.

To serve, sprinkle the parsley over the top and serve with crusty bread to mop up the dressing, if using.

Cook's tip

Provide a discarded empty half shell for each person so that they can use it as a spoon to remove the mussel from its other half shell and then eat it.

Anchovy and cheese-stuffed eggs

Huevos rellenos de anchoa y queso

Makes 16

8 eggs

1³/₄ oz/50 g canned anchovy fillets in olive oil, drained

2 oz/55 g Manchego cheese, grated

4 tbsp Spanish extra virgin olive oil

1 tbsp freshly squeezed lemon juice

1 garlic clove, crushed

4 pitted black Spanish olives, halved

4 pitted green Spanish olives, halved

hot or sweet smoked Spanish paprika, for dusting

salt and pepper

A stuffed hard-cooked egg half makes a perfect tapas dish to hold in your fingers, and although tuna is a popular fish to use for stuffing eggs, anchovies are also good, or you could use cooked shelled shrimp.

Put the eggs in a pan, then cover with cold water and slowly bring to a boil. Reduce the heat and simmer gently for 10 minutes. Immediately drain the eggs and rinse under cold running water to cool. Gently tap the eggs to crack the shells and let stand until cold.

When the eggs are cold, crack the shells all over and remove them. Using a stainless steel knife, halve the eggs, then carefully remove the egg yolks and put in a food processor.

Add the anchovy fillets, Manchego cheese, oil, lemon juice, and garlic to the egg yolks and process to a purée. Season to taste with salt and pepper.

Using a teaspoon, spoon the mixture into the egg white halves. Alternatively, using a pastry bag fitted with a ¹/₂-inch/1-cm plain tip, pipe the mixture into the egg white halves. Arrange the eggs in a serving dish, then cover and chill in the refrigerator until ready to serve.

To serve, put an olive half on the top of each stuffed egg and dust with paprika.

Cook's tip

Spanish Manchego cheese, made from the milk of sheep from La Mancha, can now be found in most supermarkets, but should you have difficulties in finding it, you could use freshly grated Parmesan cheese.

Calamari with shrimp and fava beans

Calamares con gambas y habas

Serves 4–6 as part of a tapas meal

2 tbsp Spanish olive oil

4 scallions, thinly sliced

2 garlic cloves, finely chopped

1 lb 2 oz/500 g cleaned squid bodies, thickly sliced

generous 1/3 cup dry white wine

1 lb 5 oz/600 g fresh young fava beans in their pods, shelled to give about 8 oz/225 g, or 8 oz/ 225 g frozen baby fava beans

9 oz/250 g raw jumbo shrimp, shelled and deveined

4 tbsp chopped fresh flat-leaf parsley

salt and pepper

crusty bread, to serve

In fish markets and restaurants in English-speaking countries, squid is often known by the name "calamari," from the Greek-Italian word for these cephalopods. Combining seafood with fava beans is a classic Spanish concept.

Heat the oil in a large skillet with a lid or an ovenproof casserole. Add the scallions and cook over medium heat, stirring occasionally, for 4–5 minutes, or until softened. Add the garlic and cook, stirring, for 30 seconds, or until softened. Add the squid slices and cook over high heat, stirring occasionally, for 2 minutes, or until golden brown.

Add the wine and bring to a boil. Add the fava beans and reduce the heat, then cover and simmer, for 5–8 minutes if using fresh beans or 4–5 minutes if using frozen beans, until the beans are tender.

Add the shrimp and parsley, re-cover, and simmer for an additional 2–3 minutes, or until the shrimp turn pink and start to curl. Season to taste with salt and pepper. Serve hot, with crusty bread to mop up the juices.

Cook's tip

Don't be tempted to season the squid with salt before it is cooked, as this tends to toughen it.

Fresh salmon in red bell pepper sauce

Salmón fresco en salsa de pimienta roja

Serves 6 as part of a tapas meal

2 red bell peppers
about 4 tbsp Spanish olive oil
1 lb 9 oz/700 g salmon fillets
1 onion, coarsely chopped
1 garlic clove, finely chopped
6 tbsp dry white wine
generous 1/3 cup heavy cream
salt and pepper
chopped fresh flat-leaf parsley,
to garnish
crusty bread, to serve (optional)

This is an elegant and delicious dish of fresh pink salmon drizzled with a pepper sauce. The salmon here is cut into small pieces, but it can be left as whole fillets and served with new potatoes and a green vegetable for a perfect lunch or supper dish.

Preheat the oven to 400°F/200°C. Brush the red bell peppers with 2 teaspoons of the oil and put in a roasting pan. Roast in the preheated oven for 30 minutes, then turn over and roast for an additional 10 minutes, or until the skins have blistered and blackened.

Meanwhile, remove the skin from the salmon fillets and cut the flesh into 1-inch/2.5-cm cubes. Season to taste with pepper and set aside.

Heat 2 tablespoons of the remaining oil in a large skillet, then add the onion and cook, stirring occasionally, for 5 minutes, or until softened but not browned. Add the garlic and cook, stirring, for 30 seconds, or until softened. Add the wine and bring to a boil, then let bubble for 1 minute. Remove from the heat and set aside.

When the bell peppers are cooked, using a slotted spoon, transfer to a plastic bag and let stand for 15 minutes, or until cool enough to handle.

Using a sharp knife or your fingers, carefully peel away the skin from the bell peppers. Halve the bell peppers and remove the stems, cores, and seeds, then put the flesh in a food processor.

Add the onion mixture and cream to the bell peppers and process to a smooth purée. Season to taste with salt and pepper. Pour into a pan.

Heat the remaining oil in the skillet, then add the salmon cubes and cook, turning occasionally, for 8–10 minutes, or until cooked through and golden brown on both sides. Meanwhile, gently heat the sauce in the pan.

Transfer the cooked salmon to a warmed serving dish. Drizzle over some of the bell pepper sauce and serve the remaining sauce in a small serving bowl. Serve hot, garnished with chopped parsley and accompanied by crusty bread to mop up the sauce, if using.

Vegetables
and Salads

Vegetables in Spain, unlike many other cuisines around the world, are not often served as an accompaniment but as a dish in their own right, so they make very versatile tapas dishes. Vegetables are simply combined with other ingredients to bring out their full flavor or tossed in a dressing, and salads are often served as a tapa. Potatoes, in particular, always feature prominently in a tapas selection, since they are very much part of the Spanish diet, and the recipe for Piquant potatoes is a classic.

Finally, it should be mentioned that garlic is Spain's favorite vegetable. It is used both cooked and raw to subtly flavor dishes, as in the famous garlic mayonnaise, Allioli, served with numerous tapas dishes.

Sun-dried tomato and goat cheese tarts

Tartaletas de tomate seco y queso de cabra

Makes 12

2¹/₂ oz/70 g sun-dried tomatoes in oil, drained, oil reserved, and finely chopped

1 zucchini, thinly sliced

1 garlic clove, crushed

9 oz/250 g puff pastry, thawed if frozen

5¹/₂ oz/150 g soft goat cheese

salt and pepper

Puff pastry cleverly rises to enclose the vegetables and cheese in these attractive individual tarts. The end result is very moreish, so allow for at least two per person.

Preheat the oven to 425°F/220°C. Dampen a large cookie sheet. Heat 1 tablespoon of the reserved oil from the tomatoes in a large skillet, then add the zucchini slices and cook over medium heat, stirring occasionally, for 8–10 minutes, or until golden brown on both sides. Add the garlic and cook, stirring, for 30 seconds. Remove from the heat and let cool while you prepare the pastry bases.

Thinly roll out the pastry on a lightly floured counter. Using a plain, 3¹/₂-inch/9-cm cutter, cut out 1–2 circles, rerolling the trimmings as necessary. Transfer the circles to the prepared cookie sheet and prick 3–4 times with the tines of a fork.

Divide the zucchini mixture equally between the pastry circles, add the tomatoes, leaving a ¹/₂-inch/1-cm border around the edge, and top each tart with a spoonful of goat cheese. Drizzle over 1 tablespoon of the remaining oil from the tomatoes and season to taste with salt and pepper.

Bake the tarts in the preheated oven for 10–15 minutes, or until golden brown and well risen. Serve warm.

Baby leek and asparagus salad

Ensalada de espárrago y porritos

Serves 6 as part of a tapas meal

3 eggs
1 lb/450 g baby leeks, trimmed
8 oz/225 g fresh young asparagus
spears, trimmed
2/3 cup mayonnaise
2 tbsp sherry vinegar
1 garlic clove, crushed
2 tbsp capers
salt and pepper

There is something appealing about baby vegetables, and in this case, fingers of baby leeks combine perfectly with spears of fresh young asparagus.

Put the eggs in a pan, then cover with cold water and slowly bring to a boil. Reduce the heat and simmer gently for 10 minutes. Immediately drain the eggs and rinse under cold running water to cool. Gently tap the eggs to crack the shells and let stand until cold.

Meanwhile, slice the leeks and asparagus into about 3 1/2-inch/9-cm lengths. Put both the vegetables in a pan of boiling water, then return to a boil and boil for 12 minutes, or until just tender. Drain and rinse under cold running water, then drain well.

Put the mayonnaise in a large bowl. Add the vinegar and garlic, then mix together until smooth. Season to taste with salt and pepper.

Add the leeks and asparagus to the dressing and toss together until well coated. Transfer the vegetables to a serving dish, then cover and chill in the refrigerator for at least 1 hour.

Just before serving, crack the shells of the eggs all over and remove them. Slice the eggs into quarters and add to the salad. Sprinkle over the capers and serve.

Cook's tip
If you cannot find baby leeks, or as a variation, use plump scallions instead.

Stuffed tuna and cheese bell pepper strips

Tiritas de pimienta rellenas de atún con queso

Serves 8 as part of a tapas meal

6 mixed red, green, yellow, or orange bell peppers

2 tbsp Spanish olive oil

7 oz/200 g canned tuna in olive oil, drained

scant 1/2 cup curd cheese

4 tbsp chopped fresh flat-leaf parsley

1 garlic clove, crushed

salt and pepper

Tuna, after salt cod, is Spain's most popular fish and cans of different varieties line the supermarket shelves. It makes an ideal filling for these pretty strips of colorful bell peppers.

Preheat the oven to 400°F/200°C. Brush the bell peppers with the oil and put in a roasting pan. Roast in the preheated oven for 30 minutes, then turn over and roast for an additional 10 minutes, or until the skins have blistered and blackened.

Using a slotted spoon, transfer the roasted peppers to a plastic bag and let cool for about 15 minutes, or until cool enough to handle.

Meanwhile, put the tuna on paper towels and pat dry to remove the oil. Transfer to a food processor, then add the curd cheese, parsley, and garlic and process until mixed together. Season to taste with salt and pepper.

Using a sharp knife or your fingers, carefully peel away the skins from the cooled bell peppers. Cut the bell peppers into quarters and remove the stems, cores, and seeds.

Put a heaping teaspoonful of the tuna and cheese mixture on the pointed end of each bell pepper quarter and roll up. If necessary, wipe with paper towels to remove any filling that has spread over the skins, then arrange the rolls in a shallow dish on end with the filling uppermost. Cover and chill in the refrigerator for at least 2 hours, until firm, before serving.

Eggplant tortilla wedges

Trozos de tortilla de berenjena

Serves 8–10 as part of a tapas meal

1 lb 2 oz/500 g eggplants

8 tbsp Spanish olive oil

1 onion, chopped

6 eggs

salt and pepper

chopped fresh flat-leaf parsley, to garnish (optional)

This tortilla comes from Murcia, a province on the eastern coast of Spain that is a market garden area, where eggplants are popular. Traditionally, tortilla is served cut into cubes for a tapa, but here it is cut into wedges, to be eaten with your fingers.

Cut the eggplants into ¼-inch/5-mm thick slices. Heat 2 tablespoons of the oil in a large skillet, then add the onion and cook over medium heat, stirring occasionally, for 5 minutes, or until softened but not browned.

Add the remaining oil to the skillet and heat until hot. Add the eggplant slices and cook over medium heat, turning occasionally, for 15–20 minutes until tender.

Meanwhile, lightly beat the eggs in a large bowl and season generously with salt and pepper.

When the eggplants are cooked, drain in a strainer set over a large bowl to catch the oil. When well drained, gently stir into the beaten eggs.

Wipe the skillet clean or wash, if necessary, to prevent the tortilla from sticking. Pour the reserved oil into the skillet and heat. Add the egg and eggplant mixture and cook gently for 3–4 minutes, or until the underside is just set and lightly browned. Use a spatula to loosen the tortilla away from the side and bottom of the skillet to let most of the uncooked egg run underneath and prevent the tortilla from sticking to the bottom.

Cover the tortilla with a large, upside-down plate and invert the tortilla onto it. Slide the tortilla back into the skillet, cooked-side up, and cook for an additional 3–4 minutes, or until the underside is lightly browned.

Slide the tortilla onto a warmed serving dish. Cut the tortilla into wedges and serve warm, sprinkled generously with chopped parsley to garnish, if using.

Simmered summer vegetables

Pisto

Serves 6–8 as part of a tapas meal

1 large eggplant

4 tbsp Spanish olive oil

1 onion, thinly sliced

2 garlic cloves, finely chopped

2 zucchini, thinly sliced

1 red bell pepper, cored, seeded, and thinly sliced

1 green bell pepper, cored, seeded, and thinly sliced

8 tomatoes, peeled, seeded, and chopped

salt and pepper

chopped fresh flat-leaf parsley, to garnish

slices thick country bread, to serve (optional)

This is the Spanish equivalent of the French ratatouille. As well as being served as a tapas dish, it is often served in Spain as an accompaniment to meat, poultry, or fish, or served topped with fried eggs as a light lunch or supper dish.

Cut the eggplant into 1-inch/2.5-cm cubes. Heat the oil in a large ovenproof casserole, then add the onion and cook over medium heat, stirring occasionally, for 5 minutes, or until softened but not browned. Add the garlic and cook, stirring, for 30 seconds, or until softened.

Increase the heat to medium–high, then add the eggplant cubes and cook, stirring occasionally, for 10 minutes, or until softened and beginning to brown. Add the zucchini and bell peppers and cook, stirring occasionally, for 10 minutes, or until softened. Add the tomatoes and season to taste with salt and pepper.

Bring the mixture to a boil, then reduce the heat, cover, and simmer, stirring occasionally so that the vegetables do not stick to the bottom of the pan, for 15–20 minutes, or until tender. If necessary, uncover, then increase the heat and cook to evaporate any excess liquid, as the mixture should be thick.

Serve hot or cold, garnished with chopped parsley and accompanied by bread slices for scooping up the vegetables, if using.

Cook's tip
Ideally, this is best made the day before serving, to let its flavors develop.

Deep-fried artichoke hearts

Fritura de corazones de alcachofa

Serves 4–6 as part of a tapas meal

scant 1/2 cup self-rising flour

1/4 tsp salt

1/4 tsp hot or sweet smoked Spanish paprika

1 garlic clove, crushed

5 tbsp water

1 tbsp olive oil

juice of 1/2 lemon

12 small globe artichokes

sunflower-seed or olive oil, for deep-frying

Allioli, to serve

A selection of tapas dishes often contains a deep-fried tapa. Artichokes are always a popular vegetable, but other favorites include eggplant, zucchini, broccoli, or cauliflower florets and mushrooms, all of which could be used in this recipe.

To make the batter, put the flour, salt, paprika, and garlic in a large bowl and make a well in the center. Gradually pour the water and olive oil into the well and mix in the flour mixture from the side, beating constantly, until all the flour is incorporated and a smooth batter forms. Let rest while preparing the artichokes.

Fill a bowl with cold water and add the lemon juice. Cut off the stalks of the artichokes. With your hands, break off all the leaves and carefully remove the choke (the mass of silky hairs) by pulling it out with your fingers or scooping it out with a spoon. Immediately put the artichoke hearts in the acidulated water to prevent discoloration.

Cook the artichoke hearts in a pan of boiling salted water for 15 minutes, or until tender but still firm, then drain well and pat dry with paper towels.

Heat enough sunflower-seed or olive oil in a deep-fat fryer to 350–375°F/180–190°C, or until a cube of bread browns in 30 seconds. Spear an artichoke heart on a toothpick and dip into the batter, then drop the artichoke heart and toothpick into the hot oil. Cook the artichoke hearts, in batches to avoid overcrowding, for 1–2 minutes, or until golden brown and crisp. Remove with a slotted spoon or draining basket and drain on paper towels.

Serve hot, accompanied by a bowl of Allioli for dipping.

Cook's tip

If you are unable to find fresh artichokes or would prefer not to have to prepare them, 14 oz/400 g canned artichoke hearts could be used. Drain the juices from the can and halve the artichokes if large, then dry well with paper towels before using.

Grilled zucchini salad with cilantro dressing

Ensalada de calabacín abrasado con aderezo de cilantro

Serves 6 as part of a tapas meal

1 lb 2 oz/500 g small zucchini

1 tsp salt

1 tbsp Spanish olive oil

1 garlic clove, crushed

1/3 cup pine nuts

Cilantro dressing

2 garlic cloves, chopped

1 tsp ground cumin

8 tbsp chopped fresh cilantro leaves

2 tbsp chopped fresh
flat-leaf parsley

5 tbsp Spanish extra virgin olive oil

2 tbsp white wine vinegar

salt and pepper

Often served with fish, this cilantro dressing is also known as Canary Island Green Sauce, since that is where it originated. It is also good served as a dipping sauce with boiled new potatoes.

Thinly slice the zucchini lengthwise. Layer the slices in a colander, sprinkling over a little salt, and set over a large plate. Let drain for about 1 hour.

Meanwhile, make the dressing. Put the garlic, cumin, and herbs in a food processor and, using the pulse action, process until well mixed.

With the motor running, add 1 tablespoon of the extra virgin olive oil, drop by drop. Using a spatula, scrape down the side of the bowl. With the motor running again, very slowly add the remaining oil in a thin, steady stream until it has all been incorporated and the dressing has slightly thickened.

Add the vinegar to the dressing and process for 1 minute, or until blended. Season to taste with salt and pepper.

When the zucchini have drained, quickly rinse the slices under cold running water, then dry well with paper towels or a clean kitchen towel. Put in a large bowl and add the olive oil and garlic, then toss together lightly.

Heat a ridged grill pan. Add the zucchini slices, in batches in a single layer, and cook, turning once, for 5 minutes, or until tender. Transfer to a large serving bowl. Set aside and let cool slightly.

Sprinkle the pine nuts over the zucchini. If the dressing has separated, whisk it together, then drizzle some over the zucchini. Serve the zucchini accompanied by the remaining dressing in a small serving bowl.

Cook's tip

If you do not have a ridged grill pan, the zucchini can be cooked on a flat griddle or in a large skillet, but will obviously not have the attractive markings that they have when cooked in a ridged pan.

Spanish summer salad in a tomato dressing

Ensalada estival con aderezo de tomate

Serves 8 as part of a tapas meal

4 eggs

3¹/₂ oz/100 g fine green beans

1 lb 2 oz/500 g cherry or baby plum tomatoes

1 green bell pepper, cored, seeded, and diced

1 yellow bell pepper, cored, seeded, and diced

4 small gherkins, sliced

generous ¹/₄ cup pitted black Spanish olives, halved

1 tsp capers

Tomato dressing

6 firm tomatoes

1 garlic clove, chopped

6 tbsp Spanish extra virgin olive oil

3 tbsp sherry vinegar

¹/₂ tsp hot or sweet smoked Spanish paprika

pinch of sugar

salt

Peeling tomatoes has to be the most laborious task. The joy of this recipe is that the tomatoes needed to make the dressing are grated, as the Greeks do, to remove the skins. You will be amazed at the result.

Put the eggs in a pan, then cover with cold water and slowly bring to a boil. Reduce the heat and simmer gently for 10 minutes. Immediately drain the eggs and rinse under cold running water to cool. Gently tap the eggs to crack the shells and let stand until cold.

Meanwhile, cut the beans into 1-inch/2.5-cm lengths. Cook in a pan of boiling water for 2 minutes, then drain well. Rinse under cold running water and let stand until cold.

To make the dressing, coarsely grate the tomatoes into a food processor, discarding the skins left in your hands. Add the garlic, oil, vinegar, paprika, and sugar and process until smooth. Season to taste with salt.

Put the cooled beans in a large serving bowl. Add the tomatoes and peppers and toss the vegetables together. Drizzle the dressing over the vegetables.

Sprinkle the gherkins, olives, and capers into the salad. Just before serving, crack the shells of the eggs all over and remove them. Slice the eggs into quarters and add to the salad.

Cook's tip
The flavor of the dressing is quite peppery, especially if you choose to use hot paprika. Add ¹/₄ teaspoon of paprika if a less peppery flavor suits your tastebuds.

Piquant potatoes

Patatas bravas

Serves 6 as part of a tapas meal

olive oil, for pan-frying
1 onion, finely chopped
2 garlic cloves, crushed
¼ cup white wine or dry
Spanish sherry
14 oz/400 g canned chopped
tomatoes
2 tsp white or red wine vinegar
1–2 tsp crushed dried chiles
2 tsp hot or sweet smoked
Spanish paprika
2 lb 4 oz/1 kg old potatoes
salt

A selection of tapas dishes could be said to be incomplete without a dish of *patatas bravas*! It is always a favorite, and although recipes vary, all are hot in flavor.

To make the sauce, heat 2 tablespoons of oil in a pan, then add the onion and cook over medium heat, stirring occasionally, for 5 minutes, or until softened but not browned. Add the garlic and cook, stirring, for 30 seconds. Add the wine and bring to a boil. Add the tomatoes and their juice, vinegar, chiles, and paprika, then reduce the heat and simmer, uncovered, for 10–15 minutes, or until a thick sauce forms.

When the sauce is cooked, use a hand-held blender to blend until smooth. Alternatively, transfer the sauce to a food processor and process until smooth. Return the sauce to the pan and set aside.

Do not peel the potatoes, but cut them into chunky pieces. Heat enough oil in a large skillet to come about 1 inch/2.5 cm up the side of the skillet. Add the potato pieces and cook over medium–high heat, turning occasionally, for 10–15 minutes until golden brown. Remove with a slotted spoon and drain on paper towels, then sprinkle with salt.

Meanwhile, gently reheat the sauce. Transfer the potatoes to a warmed serving dish and drizzle over the sauce. Serve hot, with wooden toothpicks to spear the potatoes.

Roasted potato wedges with shallots and rosemary

Trozos rostizados de patata con echalote y romarindo

Serves 6 as part of a tapas meal

2 lb 4 oz/1 kg small old potatoes
6 tbsp Spanish olive oil
2 fresh rosemary sprigs
5 1/2 oz/150 g baby shallots
2 garlic cloves, sliced
salt and pepper

Potato wedges have become popular in recent years, and because of their shape and size, combined with baby shallots, they make a perfect tapas dish.

Preheat the oven to 400°F/200°C. Peel and cut each potato into 8 thick wedges. Put the potatoes in a large pan of salted water and bring to a boil. Reduce the heat and simmer for 5 minutes.

Heat the oil in a large roasting pan on the stove. Drain the potatoes well and add to the roasting pan. Strip the leaves off the rosemary sprigs, then finely chop and sprinkle over the potatoes.

Roast the potatoes in the preheated oven for 35 minutes, turning twice during cooking. Add the shallots and garlic and roast for an additional 15 minutes, or until golden brown. Season to taste with salt and pepper.

Transfer to a warmed serving dish and serve hot.

Cook's tip
If you are unable to find baby shallots, larger ones can be used, but cut them in half or even quarters so that they are cooked in the time given in the recipe.

Index